Forensics in
FIRE

CONTENTS

By Dr David J. Icove

Forensics in FIRE

How Fires Begin

Fire is both our friend and our enemy and has been with us since the beginning of time. Fire occurs when a material breaks down by a chemical reaction, giving off light, heat and smoke. Fires may be so small they are barely noticeable or as large as raging forest fires.

For fires to begin and develop, four elements are necessary. There must be fuel – material that will burn. There must be enough heat so that the fuel continues to release flammable vapours. Fires also need oxygen, usually from the air, to keep them burning.

The fourth element is the chemical chain reaction that occurs when the right amounts of fuel, heat and oxygen are present. Removing one or more of these elements will put the fire out.

Fires occur whenever the conditions are right for a spark or flame to give off enough heat or energy to sustain the fire. Unsafe and fire-prone conditions in dry forests, hay fields, barns, homes, businesses and vehicles sometimes lead to disastrous and deadly fires.

Fires may be accidental, natural or intentional.

Accidental fires can occur when candles are left unattended.

Lightning strikes can hit trees or people's homes, causing naturally occurring fires.

Clarify...

sustain

intentional

?

Arsonists are people who intentionally set fires.

chemical

vapours

Where are they from?

Word Origin

Fire Investigators

Professional fire investigators find out where and how a fire started, how it progressed and what caused it to ignite. Fire investigators are usually trained in fire science. They use their knowledge and experience to investigate the causes of fires. They may also use forensic science, in which legal inquiries are tested by scientific analysis.

When a fire has been started by an arsonist, it may be the fire investigator's job to identify and arrest the person responsible. They search for items that link the criminal to the fire scene. This physical evidence may include impressions left by footprints, fingerprints or tools used to break into a building.

They may find traces of blood, along with matches, combustible liquids used to accelerate the fire, explosives or broken glass.

Sometimes people and pets do not survive fires. Fire investigators often help medical examiners find out how and why they died. Lessons learned from fatal fires can bring changes to fire codes and standards to help prevent future fires from occurring.

Inference

What can you infer about the skills a fire investigator would need to do their job?

Fire investigators work with firefighters and forensic scientists at the scene of a fire.

fire investigators at the scene of a school fire

Word Origin

accelerate

arsonist

Where are they from?

. . . sometimes people do not survive

Clarify...

ignite

combustible

analysis

Key Points	Interesting Facts
. . . fire investigators find out where and how a fire started . . . **?**	**?**

Visual Challenge
In what other ways could you present this information?

How a Fire Scene Is Reconstructed

The work of a fire investigator begins when the fire service or police have been called to a fire and have been unable to find the cause.

To discover what happened, fire investigators must reconstruct the fire scene. They have to document carefully all the complex information found at the scene. They record information about the fire, the building construction and any escape routes. They can use forensic photography, sketches and written analysis to create a picture of the scene.

They start by documenting the exterior, whether it is a building, vehicle, forest, boat or other structure. During a walk around the fire scene, a quick field search can be made for extra evidence.

The investigator can soon see the extent of fire damage and the condition of the structure, including doors and windows. They also look for any fire code violations or safety concerns. Any damage to neighbouring properties will also be noted.

Large-scale fire scenes can be photographed from an overhead crane, aerial ladder truck or aircraft.

exterior
violations
Where are they from?

Word Origin

close-up of smoke and fire damage through a doorway

Question

How do you think an aerial photograph of a fire scene could be important to a fire investigator?

An aerial view of part of a building after a fire. A fire truck with a ladder platform gives investigators an overhead perspective of the scene.

exterior photo showing fire damage to a school building

Clarify...

reconstruct

field search

?

When the exterior has been documented, it is time to move the investigation to the interior of the fire scene. Photographs and sketches are made to show what the scene looks like on arrival, before the fire debris is sifted and sorted for evidence.

Investigators then plot the damage by showing the extent and progress of the fire, including points where the fire may have started. Clues can be found in the effects of heat and smoke on different rooms, as well as damage to walls, floors, ceilings and doors. The investigators examine these solid surfaces to plot how heat has developed and flames have spread to form fire patterns. Fire patterns are often the only visible evidence left when a fire has been extinguished. They are influenced by the available fuel, ventilation and the shape and size of the room.

plume

Where's it from?

Word Origin

only visible evidence...

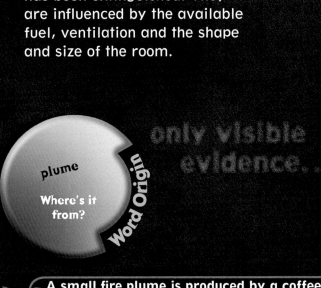

A small fire plume is produced by a coffee maker in a fire test. The fire damage on the floor, walls and ceiling is then studied by fire investigators.

The most important factor is the fire plume. This is usually a vertical column of flames, gases and smoke rising from a burning fuel source.

Fire investigators can tell where the fire started by the shape and intensity of burn patterns caused by fire plumes on floors, walls, ceilings and furniture. They can tell how intense the fire was and how it travelled. As the hot gases and smoke rise from a fire, they mix with surrounding air. The mixing zone becomes wider as hot gases rise above the fuel, forming a V pattern.

extensive damage at a fire scene showing burn patterns on furniture and walls

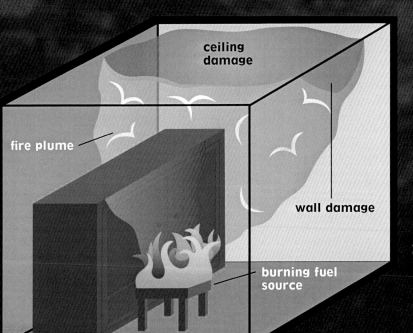

ceiling damage

fire plume

wall damage

burning fuel source

Question

Why do you think it is important that the fire scene is photographed before the debris is sifted?

The condition of window glass, which breaks during exposure to heat and fire, can also provide useful information.

Investigators also note if there were any fire alarms, smoke detectors or sprinkler systems in place that would have helped contain the fire or alerted the occupants.

Clocks can pinpoint the approximate time that they were damaged and halted by heat or power loss. The data systems in fire alarms can help reveal where and when alarms or sprinklers went off.

The weather conditions at the time of the fire can also be important, particularly high winds, changing temperatures or lightning.

Weather services and web sites keep records, such as radar images, satellite photos and surface analysis, that can assist in an investigation. For example, the location of lightning strikes is important information when deciding whether lightning caused a fire.

Witnesses can be vital for providing a full understanding of the fire. They can tell investigators about the initial stages of the fire and the weather conditions at the time. Investigators also note the position of the witnesses in relation to the fire scene. They may even walk the witnesses through the scene, if it is safe, or back to where they witnessed the fire. This can help establish the witnesses' viewpoint and jog their memories for more details.

Key Points	Interesting Facts
• The condition of window glass...can also provide useful information.	
?	?

What questions do you have about this information?

Question Generate

Visual Challenge
In what other ways could you present this information?

Question

Why do you think investigators note if there were any fire alarms, smoke detectors or sprinkler systems at the fire scene?

This window glass has melted and fractured, or "crazed", during a fire. Crazing happens when hot glass is cooled quickly, such as when water is used to put out a fire.

Clarify...

surface analysis ?

Sniffer dogs can be used to find accelerants at a fire scene.

How the Evidence Is Collected and Recorded

Fire investigators have to be very systematic, examining burn patterns and the position of evidence before it leaves the fire scene, especially when crimes are involved, such as burglary or homicide. Nothing should be moved, including the bodies of victims, until it is photographed and described in fire scene notes.

Photographs and Sketches

Investigators use a "Photograph Field Notes" form to record the description, frame and roll number of each photograph taken at the fire scene.

Aerial or perspective views of a building can reveal the overall impact of the fire, including any damage caused by extinguishing the blaze. Panoramic photographs can be used to establish what a witness might have seen or not seen from a particular location.

Sketches also help portray the fire scene and items of evidence. Fire scene sketches can provide important additional information, from rough exterior building outlines to detailed floor plans.

photographing evidence

Fire investigators have to be very systematic...
What can you infer about the job of a fire investigator?

Why do you think nothing can be moved at the fire scene at this stage?

aerial photograph of a school fire

Clarify...

systematic
frame
panoramic

?

A fire investigation officer examines burn patterns at the scene of a school fire.

Sifting the Debris

Physical evidence is sometimes called the "silent witness". It can give reliable answers to questions other investigative techniques cannot answer, and it can fill in details and support other information. Searching for physical evidence at a fire scene has to be done systematically.

Archaeologists often use a technique called gridding to help collect and document their finds. Fire investigators can use the same method as they sift through debris at a fire scene.

The scene is divided into grid squares, using rope, string or chalk. The grids are numbered in one direction and lettered in the other.

The debris is removed from each grid square and sifted, layer by layer. Recovered evidence is kept in a bag, can or envelope and labelled with the grid square's number and letter. At a later stage, the evidence can be placed back to within 30 cm of its original location. It is time-consuming and labour-intensive, but this is the best way of finding and documenting evidence, because it means the scene can be physically reconstructed after the search is complete.

Inference

Searching for physical evidence at a fire scene has to be done systematically.

What can you infer about fire investigators from this information?

Fire investigation officers work slowly and carefully.

sifting for evidence

Clarify...

distinguishable
wet sieving

same shades of white, grey or black

The evidence is measured and photographed.

Investigators also note the depth at which any evidence is found. This can be important for fires in multi-storeyed buildings where collapsed floors bury vital evidence. Sometimes fallen debris preserves evidence on lower floors. Collapsed ceilings and roofs can cover the evidence of the critical early stages of a fire.

In the ashes, all evidence seems to be the same shades of white, grey or black, and is not easily distinguishable from fire debris. Wet sieving the debris can help show up small items, such as glass, keys or jewellery, that may go unnoticed in dry ash.

How the Evidence Is Analysed

Predict: What information do you think you will find out in this chapter?

When all the physical evidence has been collected and recorded, it must be analysed scientifically. When investigators use science to analyse evidence during legal inquiries, this is known as criminalistics. Criminalistics helps to identify materials, showing what they are and where they came from. It is an important step in reconstructing events.

This physical evidence can take any form – impressions from shoes, tools, fingers, palms or feet, tissue, blood, glass, paint, soil, grease, oil, dyes, inks, documents, matches or traces of chemicals associated with fires or explosions.

Evidence may also include witness interviews, reports on injuries or post-mortems, and fire scene photographs and sketches. Criminalistics can even analyse human behaviour.

When the scene is complex or serious, such as when deaths or injuries have occurred, every possible scenario must be explored.

Fire scene diagrams similar to this one are used to help reconstruct events.

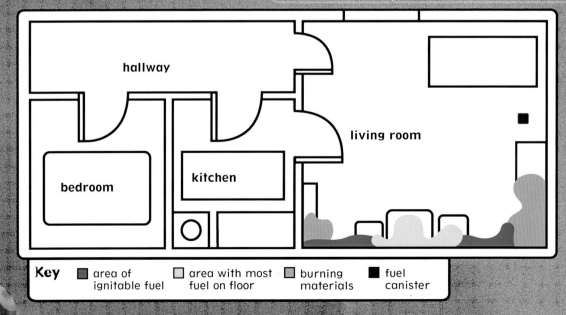

| Key | ■ area of ignitable fuel | □ area with most fuel on floor | ▢ burning materials | ■ fuel canister |

Evidence from a serious fire
is processed in a laboratory.

physical evidence can take any form

Key Points	Interesting Facts
When all the physical evidence has been collected and recorded, it must be analysed scientifically. **?**	**?**

Inference

Criminalistics
can even analyse
human behaviour.

**What can you
infer about
criminalistics
from this text?**

Visual Challenge
In what other ways could you present this information?

Clarify...

distribution

laboratories

?

sequence

Where's it from?

Word Origin

A forensic scientist takes samples from a suspect's clothing for DNA analysis.

...link a person to a scene

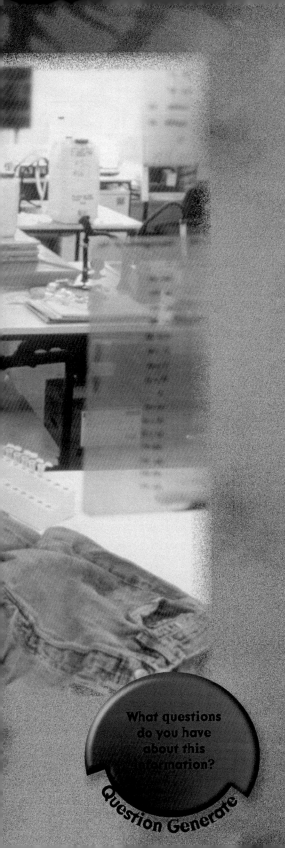

For example, an investigator arrives at a fire scene to find an unlatched door with its window broken and blood smears – all visible evidence. The reconstruction of this evidence would be that the door was originally locked and its window broken by an intruder. This is shown by the glass fracture patterns caused by a blow from the outside. The intruder would have cut themselves on the glass and, while fumbling for the lock and latch, left blood smears on the door.

Analysis of the blood, or any fingerprints left on the door, glass or latch, could identify the intruder. Glass found on a suspect's clothing could be compared to window glass from the door to confirm a two-way transfer – the suspect's blood to the scene and glass from the scene to the suspect. The distribution of cuts or abrasions, along with glass fragments, would confirm the suspect's method of entry.

Criminalistics laboratories help in the reconstruction of scenes and events, testing ideas about what happened, where, when and in what sequence. They can also link a suspect to a scene or fire victim, and link a scene to a suspect or their vehicle.

What questions do you have about this information?

Question Generate

Crime laboratories can analyse a wide variety of physical evidence.

Impression Evidence

When the pattern or texture of an object is imprinted onto another object, it provides impression evidence. A shoe leaving an impression in soft clay outside a window, or the ragged edge of a hatchet blade leaving a striated, rough cut on wood are examples of impression evidence.

A dusty shoe can leave an identifiable print on a clean surface, and a clean shoe can remove dust from a dirty surface and leave the same information.

...common form of impression evidence

Shoeprints are a common form of impression evidence. Whenever possible, the object bearing the impression is sent to the lab or, if it can't be removed, investigators send photos or make a cast of the impression for analysis.

Shoeprints can show where someone entered or left a room or building, where he or she went and in what sequence. If two or more people were there, shoeprints can establish which people went where in the building.

Shoeprints on doors that have been kicked in may be made clearer by the fire. Special chemicals can be used to show up the shoe impressions on paper or cardboard. Shoeprints can also be found in soil, dust or blood.

Question

How do you think impression evidence could be important at a fire scene?

A forensic scientist measures a shoeprint taken from a suspect's shoe.

Clarify...

imprinted
striated
cast

Prints from fingers, palms and feet can survive fires. A finger, palm or foot touching a clean surface, such as glass or metal, can leave a person's prints. Almost invisible oils, fats and sweat secretions can be transferred from the skin to the surface, along with grease or paint. These prints are often called latent because they require treatment to make them visible and recordable. Fingerprints in blood can be enhanced by special sprays to make them readable.

These fresh prints can then be compared to previously recorded prints. Databases of reference prints, taken from non-criminals as well as criminals, and powerful computers have made it possible to scan millions of recorded prints quickly to make a shortlist of possible matches.

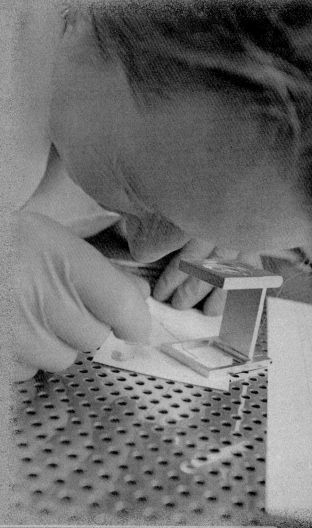

A forensic scientist counts the ridges on a fingerprint pattern. Since no two people have the same fingerprints, they are an important part of criminalistics.

Do you think there should be fingerprint databases? Why or why not?

Opinion

... prints can survive fires ...

Key Points	Interesting Facts
Prints from fingers, palms and feet can survive fires.	
?	?

Visual Challenge
In what other ways could you present this information?

fingerprints revealed on a glove that has been dusted with magnetic powder

Trace Evidence

Trace evidence is the remains of soil, glass, paint chips, metal fragments, chemicals, hairs and fibres that may cling to the shoes or clothing of a suspect. Liquids may also soak into the clothing or remain on the bottom of the suspect's shoes. When hairs and fibres are discovered at a fire scene, investigators take samples from victims or suspects for comparison. Samples of flammable and combustible liquids can help pinpoint what started a fire. These samples are all carefully packaged and labelled and sent to the laboratory for analysis.

Photographs and Sketches

Photographs can also be examined at forensic laboratories. Photogrammetry is a process that gathers information from photographs. It can accurately measure distances between key features in photographs taken at a fire scene. For example, the actual walking distance between a deceased victim in a bed and the doorway may be crucial in an investigation.

Fire scene sketches allow the investigator to show the relationships between objects that cannot be captured in photographs. Items may lie in separate rooms, under or behind large furniture, or be visible only from overhead or via cross-section.

Sometimes many sketches are made of the same view to show separate kinds of evidence. One sketch could show plume damage and another the location of samples of evidence. Computer-aided drafting (CAD) can provide two- and three-dimensional sketches that are often used as courtroom exhibits.

Fibres can be compared under a microscope.

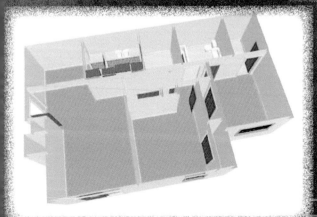

Clarify...

crucial

?

A forensic scientist uses a suction device to collect trace evidence from the seat of a car.

fire scene photograph of a kitchen after a fire

Question

In what ways do you think a fire investigator would take care when collecting evidence?

What questions do you have about this information?

Question Generate

CAD sketch of a house floor plan

The Story Comes Together

Little by little, all the pieces of information come together to reconstruct a fire. From that first phone call, when the fire investigator is brought to the scene, a huge amount of work is involved – photography, interviews, sifting and documentation of evidence and then careful laboratory analysis.

And the story does not end there. Court cases, insurance claims and people's futures all depend on the accuracy of the work of fire investigators and criminalistic laboratories.

Key Points	Interesting Facts
?	?

Visual Challenge
In what other ways could you present this information?

Index

Fire investigators perform a fire test on a house.

Think about the Text

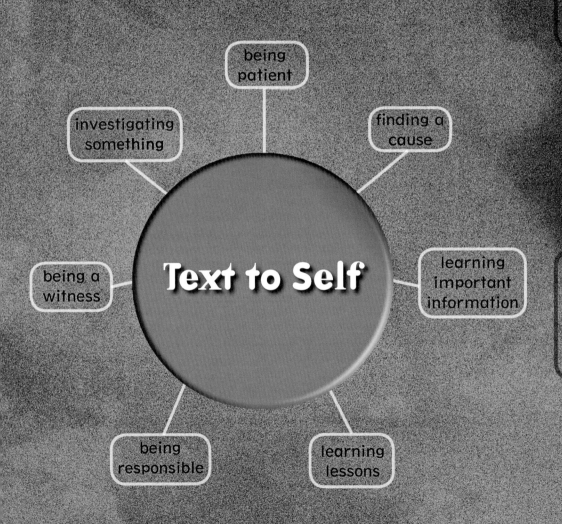

being patient

investigating something

finding a cause

being a witness

Text to Self

learning important information

being responsible

learning lessons

Text to Text

Talk about other informational texts you may have read that have similar features. Compare the texts.

Text to World

Talk about situations in the world that might connect to elements in the text.

Planning an Informational Explanation

1 Select a topic that explains why something is the way it is or how something works.

2 Make a mind map of questions about the topic.

How do fires begin?

Why are fire investigators called to a fire scene?

How is the evidence analysed?

Forensics in Fire

How is a fire scene reconstructed?

How is the evidence collected and recorded?

3 Locate the information you will need.

Library

Internet

Experts

4 Organise your information using the questions you selected as headings.

5 Make a plan.

Introduction:

Fire occurs when a material breaks down by a chemical reaction, giving off light, heat and smoke.

Points in a coherent and logical sequence:

Fire Investigators → How a Fire Scene Is Reconstructed → How the Evidence Is Collected and Recorded

How the Evidence Is Analysed → The Story Comes Together

6 Design some visuals to include in your explanation. You can use graphs, diagrams, labels, charts, tables, cross-sections . . .

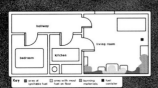

Writing an Informational Explanation

Have you . . .

- explored causes and effects?

- used scientific and technical vocabulary?

- used the present tense? (Most explanations are written in the present tense.)

- written in a formal style that is concise and accurate?

- avoided unnecessary descriptive details, metaphors or similes?

- avoided author bias or opinion?

Don't forget to revisit your writing.
Do you need to change, add or delete
anything to improve your explanation?